Texas
Wineries

Texas Wineries

by
Melinda Esco

TCU Press
Fort Worth ★ Texas

★ A TEXAS SMALL BOOK ™

Copyright © 2009 by Melinda Esco

Library of Congress Cataloging-in-Publication Data

Esco, Melinda.
Texas wineries / Melinda Esco.
p. cm.
"A Texas Small Book.™"
ISBN 978-0-87565-396-9
(casebound laminate : alk. paper)
1. Wine and wine making—Texas—History.
2. Wineries—Texas—Guidebooks.
3. Texas—Guidebooks. I. Title.
TP557.E83 2009
641.2'209764--dc22

2009021306

TCU Press
P. O. Box 298300
Fort Worth, Texas 76129
817.257.7822
http://www.prs.tcu.edu

To order books: 800.826.8911

Printed in China by Everbest Printing Company through
Four Colour Imports, Ltd, Louisville, Kentucky

Design/Margie Adkins Graphic Design

Dedication

I dedicate this book to my delightful dad, Benny McElroy,
who made wine in the kitchen cabinet when I was a teen
and to my wonderful mom, Billye McElroy, who let him.

Contents

Introduction

This is a small book about a large topic, a glimpse at the Texas wine industry. And like Lyle Lovett's band, Sam Houston's statue, and Big Bend's mountains, winemaking in Texas is large. This agricultural-based tourism phenomenon is Texas big business at its best.

Writing this book was an assignment from Judy Alter, director and acquisitions editor of TCU Press. She is also my boss. My idea for it began on a trip home with my husband after visiting my mother-in-law in Bangs. Mark took a right turn at the little sign, which we had passed probably a hundred times, for the Rising Star Vineyards on Highway 183 just north of the town after which it is named. We followed the caliche road going east and a dust cloud followed us. A typically beautiful Texas ranch with big oak trees and row after row of grapevines soon appeared. We reached the modest but inviting entryway to the winery only fifteen minutes before closing time on a Sunday afternoon, and owner Michael Ourbre warmly welcomed us in for a tasting. I took the offer (Mark doesn't drink wine—this became important to me during the course of this project) and ended up buying a couple of bottles and a few other gifts from a wonderful selection of wine-themed goodies for sale in the front room. On the way home I decided that

Rising Star Vineyards, Rising Star

1

Texas wineries would be the perfect topic for a book in our Texas Small Books™ series. I even had an author in mind. But when I brought it up for discussion at the next staff meeting Judy told me she wanted me to write it.

"Me?" I questioned. "But I'm not a wine snob."

"You mean you don't sniff the cork?" asked editor Susan Petty.

"Correct," I laughed.

But I do like to drink wine. And quickly I realized that this would mean taking road trips all over the state—one of my favorite things to do. So, what began as a task that I was initially reluctant to tackle suddenly morphed into a challenge that I couldn't resist. Talk about a good gig!

I wasted no time on my ambitious plan to visit every winery in Texas that I possibly could. I think that's the real reason I got the assignment—Judy acknowledges my passion for traveling around Texas, and I think she figured I would be willing to make it a mission. That very weekend on a trip to a friend's sixtieth birthday party at his home close to Elgin, Mark and I, with friends in tow, hit six wineries in the Hill Country in less than twenty-four hours. We mapped our route and upon leaving Spillerville (outside Marble Falls) we visited Spicewood Vineyards and Stone House Vineyard near Spicewood, Texas Hills Vineyard close to Johnson City, Driftwood Vineyards and Mandola Estate Winery in

Patio at
Spicewood Vineyards
near Spicewood

Driftwood, and Three Dudes Winery in San Marcos. The fun had begun. But, early on I realized that writing this little book was going to get expensive. And since I am the production manager at TCU Press and responsible for the book budget, I figured out that the royalties I'll be making will barely cover that first trip even if the entire print run sells out. Yikes! When the price of gasoline soared to almost $4.00 per gallon I became fully aware that it would be prohibitive for me to visit all of the wineries in Texas. But it was sure fun trying.

I discovered all sorts of interesting things about wine during my research for this book—no, it wasn't all just about getting a wine buzz. I'm still far from being a wine expert but I learned something about everything from bouquets and barrels to varietals and viticultures, and I studied up on the history of winemaking in Texas. I learned new vocabulary words, how to taste wine, and the proper way to serve it. I even figured out why I should sniff the cork. I also read about how to describe wines. But characterizations of the different tastes and smells of the whites, the reds, and the blushes are confusing to me. I don't get analyses like "nuance over force" or "bold yet unassuming." And I feel a little silly trying to make up my own. Describing wine actually reminds me of Mad Libs™—remember those word games our kids had in the '90s that listed a number of words that you could use to fill in the blanks in sentences to come up with zany

Patio at Stone House Vineyard near Spicewood

combinations? I prefer to keep it simple with my observations. "Good or not so good? Do I like this wine or don't I?" That's why this book does not include my personal comments about the wines I tasted, even though I enjoyed a number of them and brought several home. I leave that to wine expert Wes Marshall, author of *The Wine Roads of Texas: An Essential Guide to Texas Wines and Wineries* (Maverick Publishing Company, San Antonio, Texas). In his book he not only maps out road trips that highlight just about every winery in the state, he shares anecdotes about his visits and expresses his highly cultivated opinion of the wines. Rather, I'm hoping that this small book teaches you a thing or two about wine, encourages you to try Texas wine if you haven't, motivates you to visit a winery or two (or every one of them in the state if you can afford to), or perhaps inspires you to approach the wine industry as a business opportunity.

During my many visits to wineries on this year long grape junket I met some wonderful people who make a living from winemaking. Texas winery owners come from a multitude of backgrounds, and their stories are intriguing. They are doctors, bankers, pharmacists, engineers, inventors, farmers, retired military, and one is even a former NASA payload specialist. For many it's a family affair, and often a multigenerational one. Tommy and Linda Kaye Qualia operate

View overlooking the Driftwood Vineyards during winter

6

the Val Verde Winery that his grandfather, Frank, began more than a hundred years ago. Twin brothers Bill (Texas Legato) and Gill (Pillar Bluff Vineyards) Bledsoe operate complimentary yet competing wineries within hollering distance of each other in Lampasas. The Three Dudes are a two-friend-and-family-member combo (and their wives—the three dudettes) turned business partners. Some have deep Texas roots while others have lived all over the world. One thing I found common, though, among the many fabulous folks I met was their enthusiasm for the wine business. I'm of the impression that it's just as much fun as it is work. But I understand that it's also serious business. And Texas understands this, too. The wine business in this state brings in more than one billion dollars annually. At publication there are more than 160 wineries currently operating here. Winemaking is the umbrella that covers a range of business operations: agriculture, manufacturing, sales, and probably the most profitable sector, tourism. And then there's advertising, marketing, printing, event planning, and the list goes on.

Oak trees at Mandola Estate Winery near Driftwood

Wine begins with the grape, or I should say with the fruit—wine can be processed from just about any fruit but this book is about grape wine. Grapes grow in a wide variety of soils but they require proper irrigation and good drainage. The soil and climate in which grapes are grown impacts them so significantly that even grapes of the same variety can taste

9

different depending upon the region where they grow. Texas is so big that there are eight appellations or regions recognized as federally designated viticultures. This translates into hundreds of Texas wines—all different. Not every winery grows its own grapes. And not all of the vineyards operate wineries. There is a huge market for Texas-grown grapes and the crops are quite valuable.

In addition to the enterprising agriculture industry that winemaking in Texas supports, many other businesses profit from wine. More than one winery owner I met told me that "winemaking is tourism." Not only are there wineries within an afternoon's drive from just about everywhere in the state, there are a number of wine festivals and on-site events that often include music and food. Many of the wineries boast fancy restaurants or provide catering and serve as the perfect location for

Margaret Collins serving wine at the La Bodega Winery inside the terminal at DFW International Airport.

parties, weddings, and receptions. Several host holiday events in December and for New Year's or Valentine's Day, as well as plan driving tours that include day trips and overnighters. There are small wineries, medium-sized wineries, and large ones in the most idyllic Texas settings. There's even one inside DFW Airport! I've run across winery owners or their employees serving wine at various public events from Fort Worth's Gallery Night to the Marfa Lights Festival. Wineries are currently a popular topic for magazines and newspapers because not only is such writing about wine, it's also about food. And writing about food is as good a gig as writing about wine. Good Texas food and wine pairings bring out the best in both.

In case you do decide to visit all of them, I've included, beginning on page 59, a listing of every winery in the state conducting business at publication time. There is also a glossary of terms that starts on page 79. Keep this Texas Small Book™ in the car to take on road trips. I am really hoping you will go ahead and take the turn the next time you see a sign for a winery. Stop in to taste the different wines, linger for a while, or buy a bottle to take home. Meet the people, take in the scenery, and enjoy yourself. ★

A Brief History

For centuries grapes have grown wild in Texas. Fifteen native species grow here giving Texas the distinction of claiming more native species than anywhere in the world. In the 1600s Spanish missionaries, with vines they brought from Mexican missions, planted grapes near the Rio Grande close to present-day El Paso thus establishing the first vineyard at the Ysleta Mission. But to many early Texas settlers grape growing was unfamiliar. As Europeans from wine-producing countries began settling in Texas in the 1800s they brought grapevine cuttings with them, and they planted the rootstock on their newly acquired land. A number of these imported grapes grew for a while but the vines eventually died and only the native varieties survived.

Back in Europe, vineyards were almost completely wiped out during the 1840s; the catastrophe was ultimately traced to a deadly fungus named oidium. For replacements, many of the European vintners planted labrusca rootstock that they imported from the new world because of the vines' resistance to this destructive form of powdery mildew. Although these fungus-resistant vines thrived for several years, they eventually began to die out during the 1860s. In 1868 the French discovered that these labrusca vines they thought would

Vines at Lost Creek Vineyards near Lake LBJ

13

save their vineyards actually carried a deadly parasite named phylloxera. By the time these tiny lice were identified nearly all the vineyards in France were lost.

Texas actually played a role in helping save the French wine industry. Sort of an irony considering the opinion held by some people that Texas wine is inferior to French wine. Here's the story: Illinois native Thomas Volney Munson (1843-1913) graduated from the University of Kentucky in Lexington, earned a master of science degree from the State Agricultural and Mechanical College of Kentucky, and worked at the university as a science professor in 1870-71. In 1873 he moved to Nebraska and began his career as a horticulturist and viticulturist. It was his passion for grape growing that motivated him to experiment with the native wild grapes of the area when he noticed that these vines were not as susceptible to disease as the European vinifera. But the weather extremes in Nebraska hampered his efforts to grow disease-resistant rootstocks, so in 1876 he moved to the North Texas town of Denison, where his brothers were already living. Munson quickly recognized the enormous diversity of soil and climate around Texas so he began traveling extensively throughout the state to collect native varieties of grapes. His research led him to write a number of articles on the classification and hybridization of grapes. Much of his work concentrated on improving American grapes, and his studies eventually led to the introduction of more than 300 grape varieties. Munson became an authority on growing grapes, and the French vintners contacted him for help. He shipped them phylloxera-resistant rootstock to graft with European varieties. It worked. The vines thrived and eventually the European wine industry regained lost ground. For his efforts Munson received the French Legion of Honor Chevalier du Merite Agricole. Texas authors Sherrie S. McLeRoy and Roy E. Renfro, Jr., PhD, chronicled Munson's life in their award-winning book, *Grape Man of Texas* (Eakin Press, Austin, Texas). McLeRoy and Renfro received the 2005 Gourmand World Cookbook Award for "Best Wine Book in the World."

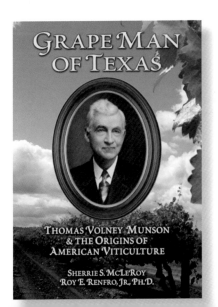

Revised edition of McLeRoy and Renfro's book *Grape Man of Texas*. Courtesy of the Wine Appreciation Guild

15

The Texas wine industry grew in the late 1800s, and by the turn of the century as many as twenty-five wineries operated in the state. But in 1919, passage of the Volstead Act, the eighteenth amendment to the Constitution of the United States, established Prohibition outlawing the production and sale of alcoholic beverages nationwide. After that, only one Texas winery survived: the Val Verde Winery which was established by Frank Qualia in 1883 near the border of Mexico in Del Rio. Originally from Italy, Qualia moved to Mexico when he was eighteen years old and after a short time south of the border he ended up in San Antonio. It was there that he heard that land was available on this side of the Rio Grande so

he moved to Del Rio and acquired some fertile property through a land development program. He farmed various crops including grapes. What began as winemaking for family and friends eventually turned into a commercial venture. During Prohibition, Qualia continued to grow grapes and his vineyard was able to survive the ban on alcohol by selling table grapes.

It wasn't until 1933 when Prohibition was repealed by another amendment to the Constitution that the wine industry got a new start. But it still took years for Texas to make a comeback. Even after the repeal of Prohibition there were still many laws on the books governing the sale and distribution of alcohol that hindered the industry. In fact, today, there are a number of Texas counties or parts of counties that remain "dry," where the sale of alcohol is prohibited. In the meantime, vineyards in California were thriving and that state began to rival the European vintners by improving their skills as winemakers to produce good wines. When the California wines began winning in international competitions, people began to notice.

In 1971, Dr. Bobby Smith, an Arlington osteopathic physician, bought fifty acres of land near Springtown in Parker county and planted a vineyard that next year. A few years later, the Llano Estacado Winery just outside Lubbock began operations. The Shady Lake Growers Association was formed, and a new generation of Texas wineries was born. Texas

Exterior of tasting room at La Buena Vida Vineyards at Springtown

17

Llano Estacado Winery next to the cotton fields near Lubbock

law, however, needed changes in order to support winemaking as an industry. It was illegal for Smith to make wine in Springtown. Unable to afford a lobbyist, he spearheaded a group that eventually influenced the legislature to pass the Texas Farm Winery Act of 1977, which enabled grape growers to produce wine in a dry county as long as the distribution of the wine itself took place where it was legal to do so. When then-governor Dolph Briscoe asked what the bill was supposed to do he was simply told that it was going to help the grape farmers. He signed it. However, legislation didn't go quite far enough, and many growers encountered further legal roadblocks. For example, Texas wineries that operated in dry counties still could not sell wine from their tasting rooms. And it just so happened that a number of the state's

18

best vineyards were in dry areas. Smith bought property in nearby Lakeside just inside Tarrant County where it was legal to sell alcohol. He opened a tasting room there but he had to establish it as another business so he could legally sell the wine he made in Springtown to the tasting room he ran in Lakeside. Mark and I visited his La Buena Vida Tasting Room back in the 1980s before he had to sell it to the state for the expansion of Highway 199.

In 2001 laws changed again. Susan Combs, then-commissioner of the Texas Department of Agriculture (TDA), was instrumental in shepherding through the state legislature the successful passage of laws that paved the way for Texas wineries to profit. It finally became legal in dry counties for wineries to sell wine in their tasting rooms and to ship wine to or from dry or wet areas. After subsequent years of appeals and legal wrangling, customers can now place their orders with any winery in the state and pick them up at approved package stores. Or they can drive out to Springtown on the weekend, buy it there and visit with Smith. He also sells the most delicious cheese that he makes from a recipe handed down from his mother. Bobby Smith has been a business associate and friend of my parents for more than thirty years, and he delivers his wine to them by the caseload. I've been fortunate to be on the receiving end of many bottles of La Buena Vida wine! ★

Luz de Estrella
Winery between
Alpine and Marfa

Big Business

Everything is bigger in Texas, and the wine industry is certainly no exception. The Lone Star State currently claims distinction as the fifth-largest wine-producing state in the country, after California, New York, Washington, and Oregon. More than 8,000 people are employed in some aspect of the wine business, and the industry pours over a billion dollars a year into the Texas economy. The wine business in Texas is as much about tourism as it is about the grapes on the vine or the wine in the bottle. Wine events across the state range from intimate dinners and afternoon concerts to driving tours and two-day festivals. Sometimes the wineries work together offering opportunities to tourists where they can taste a number of wines from the different wineries in a single setting. Some of the larger wineries include bed and breakfasts (B&Bs), like Messina Hof near College Station, and a number of them also support restaurants that serve up fabulous dishes to accompany their wines. As Gladys and Raymond Haak, owners of the Santa Fe vineyard and winery bearing their last name, put it, "we're in the entertainment business." In addition to hosting Sunday afternoon concerts during the summer, they have their grapevines blessed by a priest and they invite the public to help them harvest. The Lightcatcher Winery, near Lake Worth, holds an annual Crush Day, a delightful celebration where Lucy look-alikes (including a few hilarious-looking males) pay homage to comedienne Lucille Ball's infamous *I Love Lucy* grape-stomping episode. The people in this state have embraced wine as a cultural celebration that brings together nature and humanity in the most creative of ways. After having visited a number of wineries around the state I can attest that tourism at Texas wineries is alive and well.

Singing Water Vineyards, outside Comfort

Winemaking is an expensive venture. Big-time expensive. The initial step is deciding whether to grow your grapes (thus becoming a farmer in addition to running a business) or to buy grapes from outside sources and concentrate instead on building and operating a winery. This business decision affects all the rest: the location and the size of the winery; what to include—a tasting room, an events center, a restaurant, or a B&B; which grapes to grow, which wines to make, how to market them; and so on and so on. It takes deep pockets to finance a winery, and that is a scary prospect when you consider the risks involved. Bottom line is that you have to have grapes to make wine whether you grow them yourself or purchase them from other growers. As many a Texas farmer can testify, in all likelihood, at one time or another, the crops are going to fail. Whether due to pestilence, disease, extreme weather conditions, or feral hogs, crop failure in Texas is a certainty—a fact I've grown up knowing. But scary or not, it's never stopped Texans before, and it's not stopping the state's vintners now.

I've been just about everywhere in Texas, having lived here all my life. I particularly enjoy treks through the Hill Country, but my favorite place in the state to explore is Big Bend. You can see the Luz de Estrella Vineyards from the road on Highway 90 just east of Marfa. For those not familiar with the area, Marfa is about a hundred miles to the north of Big Bend Ranch State Park and Big Bend National Park. This unique little town, the seat of Presidio County, is famous for its artists, for being the set location of the 1950s epic movie *Giant,* and for the mystical phenomenon known as the

"Marfa Lights"—lights from an unexplained source that appear and move about in the sky on some nights. And yes, I've witnessed them on more than one occasion. They are visible from the winery whose name is Spanish for "starlight" so you can make arrangements to go to the winery for an enchanting evening that includes a bottle of wine and a front row seat to this mysterious show.

But many of the vineyards in the Hill Country are hidden from the main road, tucked away behind hills, across creeks, and up and down roads that wind around before revealing spectacularly scenic views. One thing to note is that although most of the maps showing the location of wineries (particularly

Fountain at La Buena Vida at Grapevine

Patio at Torre di
Pietra Winery near
Fredericksburg

1880s log cabin at
Becker vineyards
near Fredericksburg

the ones published by the TDA)
are quite accurate, often the signs
pointing the way are difficult
to spot. At least they were
for me. This isn't true in
every case but you have
to watch
closely
to

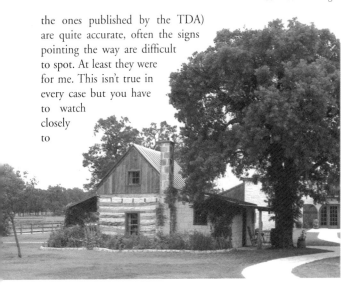

Entryway to Grape
Creek near Stonewall

notice some of the signs from the road—
especially if you're driving sixty miles an hour.
And good luck if you have to ask anyone in
Comfort how to get to the Singing Water
Vineyards located on Mill Dam Road, about
five miles southwest of there. It is a gorgeous
drive from the historic district in town out
to the winery, crossing a cool spot on the
Guadalupe River and passing an old cemetery,
but not one of the locals whom we asked for
directions could help us find our way. The
drive is well worth the effort as it is for many of
the wineries in other areas of the state as well.

Some of the wineries are located right in the middle of town, like Brennan Vineyards in Comanche or La Buena Vida Vineyards at Grapevine and Homestead Winery at Grapevine, both just a few blocks and within walking distance of the town's historic Main Street. But most wineries are just outside of cities or towns and visiting them is an adventure. Whatever the location, each Texas winery definitely has its own character.

Metal sculpture at Homestead Winery at Grapevine

After reaching the winery destination of choice, you'll find that many encourage visitors to linger outdoors. In addition to attractive garden settings, there may be an elaborate wooden deck or a patio paved in stone, a simple open pole barn covered by a tin roof, or a rustic arbor shaded by grapevines. A number of them are as beautiful outside as they are inside, like the Torre di Pietra Winery near Fredericksburg, with its substantial sandstone fireplace and patios accented with native plantings; or neighboring Becker Vineyards, with its nineteenth-century limestone barn, log cabin, and acres of lavender that grow next to the vineyard. I love

Doorway at Cap*Rock Winery near Lubbock

27

seeing the way the grapevines grow, all in rows holding hands in solidarity, their thick woody stems looking as if they are trying to twist their way to freedom from the tethers that force them to stay put. Whether the vines are flush with grapes or it is the time of year they stand stark in their nakedness, they are simply beautiful. Keep that in mind if you're wondering whether to visit a winery during the winter months. With outdoor fireplaces and heaters it's a great time to visit. Another treat at many wineries is the outdoor sculpture. This tell me loud and clear that the wine business is all about the arts. And no wonder the wineries do so well hosting concerts—these celebrations of art, music, and wine are a feast for the senses.

For many of the adventurous entrepreneurs who have built successful wineries (and there are plenty around the state) their business model includes a tasting room. I found that no matter the size of the winery, each tasting room is unique in its design and its offerings. Some wineries

Sue Lynn Bledsoe enjoying serving customers at her family's Texas Legato near Lampasas charge a fee to taste their wines, as much as six dollars for four controlled pours. Often, the ones that do charge will deduct the amount of the fee from the price if you purchase a bottle of wine. But a number of the wineries give free tastings, and sometimes they serve cheese and crackers or chocolate, not only to cleanse the palate before switching to a different wine but also to highlight how their wines pair with food. Or to offer good ol' Texas hospitality. Many of the winery owners themselves serve the wines for tasting. This one-on-one contact is the perfect opportunity for both customer and winemaker to learn about each other. That relationship is important for success in the business, and it's interesting to meet the owners. Their enthusiasm and passion for the business is evident and inspiring—they've each traveled a different path but they all share a common destination. The first time we visited the Bluff Dale Vineyards, my wine-touring friend Barbara Stevenson and I connected instantly to Theresa Hayes who, along with husband David, owns and operates this North

David and Theresa Hayes, owners of Bluff Dale Vineyards off Hwy 377 near Bluff Dale

Bar at Fall Creek
Vineyards near Tow

Texas winery. We introduced ourselves and in
a matter of minutes the three of us were wiping
tears from our eyes before Mark barely had time
to make it in from the car. But some of the
larger wineries, of course, must hire employees
to help. We enjoyed talking with the adorable
college coeds serving at the elegant and massive
Mandola Estate Winery—what a fun part-time
job! And Judy and I had a good laugh watching
the kids working at Messina Hof whose mission
it was to carry an enormous empty wine barrel
up a double staircase to the second floor above
the restaurant. Whether it's the owner or an
employee who is pouring, it is most important
that the server is knowledgeable about the wines
and that the customers feel welcome when they
walk in the door.

A number of the tasting rooms showcase fine woodworking and superior masonry skills with their elaborate bars, intricate wine racks, and rock fireplaces. The bar is the nexus of a tasting room. If there are 160-plus different wineries in Texas then there are that many bars. And if you can't find at least one of them that you can belly up to and feel comfortable then I don't know what to say. Often the bar itself has its own legend—now that's Texan! Since Mark is a masonry contractor and has built many a fine fireplace, I'm drawn to them—as much for the essence and beauty of the fireplace itself as

Fireplace at Torre di Pietra Winery near Fredercksburg

for the warmth it provides. So, I am particularly fond of the wineries that include them.

Most of the tasting rooms offer comfortable seating surrounded by inspiring artwork like the painting hanging above the fireplace at Fall Creek Vineyards near Tow or the hand-carved Belgian altar at Chisholm Trail Winery west of Fredericksburg. The architecture of the different wineries is as varied as Texans themselves. From the romantic Tuscan feel of Torre di Pietra to the German-style limestone barn at Becker or the minimalist Stone House (that, by the way, has a gorgeous women's restroom) to the historic former cotton gin that houses Sister Creek

Tasting room at Fall Creek Vineyards near Tow

32

Barrel display at
Llano Estacado
Winery near
Lubbock

Vineyards, none are the same. Just like the wines
they serve.

Another benefit of this exploration is that
I found the perfect solution for those of us who
don't like to Christmas shop at the mall: winery
gift shops. There's something for everyone on
your list (okay, maybe not for the kids or babies
you buy for) but there are definitely some fun
gifts for adults, from T-shirts and fancy wine
gadgets to the wine itself that can be custom
packaged in the most elaborate presentations.
And for family or friends who don't drink wine

there are the cheese trays. I kept noticing that many of the gift shops carry these nifty glass trays that look like a collapsed wine bottle. It wasn't until I visited with Annette Mainz at Sister Creek that I learned Texas law prohibits a winery from packaging its wine in previously used bottles. So, someone came up with the bright idea to recycle the bottles by fashioning them into nice serving trays for cheese and crackers—a good way to go green. Guess what I'll be giving for Christmas gifts this year!

Many wineries conduct tours of their operations to share with the public how they make their wine. I toured several and even though the setup of each was different the winemaking process was basically the same. Mark and I enjoyed our personal tour (because we were the only two people there in line for the 11:00 A.M. tour) by Adam Bielamowicz at Llano Estacado Winery outside Lubbock. They have a huge, impressive operation with large machinery and equipment, a laboratory with scientists making the wine, a massive barrel room, and even a museum-quality exhibit showing how the barrels are made and where corks come from. Barbara and I escorted each other on the self-guided tour at Sister Creek that consisted of two small rooms that house huge steel vats and oak barrels and a table where the wine is bottled. Owners Bob and Linda Armstrong at Luz de Estrella not only gave us a thoroughly informative session on winemaking, but we visited with them while they were busy packaging several bottles to fill an order. While planning a trip to Big Bend I looked into making arrangements to tour Ste. Genevieve Wines in Fort Stockton only to find out tourists aren't really welcome. Not that the people there are rude or anything, but the winery is open to the public only occasionally and you have to check with the Fort Stockton Chamber of Commerce to see about arranging a tour. It's a commercial winery venture between Mesa Vineyards owned by Pat Prendergast, who bottles the wine and the University of Texas that owns the vineyard, the largest in the state covering more than 900 acres. Tourism is not the focus of Ste. Genevieve. But making

Barrel room at Sister Creek Vineyards near Sisterdale

good wine is because this winery outsells all other Texas wineries.

Back to the ones that do rely on tourism—on any given weekend there may be a concert or a special dinner hosted by one of the wineries. Some sponsor seasonal tours like the Fredericksburg Wine Road 290 Ragin Cajun event, a forty-five-mile stretch of road that highlights nine wineries between Johnson City and just west of Fredericksburg. Each venue offers a free taste of Cajun food and a set of souvenir Mardi Gras beads. The eight Way Out Wineries (Alamosa Wine Cellars, Barking Rocks Winery, Bluff Dale Vineyards, Brennan Vineyards, Pillar Bluff Vineyards, Red Caboose Winery, Rising Star Vineyards, and Texas Legato) host three-day road trip events several times during the year. There are also numerous wine festivals. Grapefest, probably the state's largest one, is held annually in September in Grapevine over several days and thousands of people attend.

The TDA is helping to market wineries with a Web site, event support, and fun things like the Texas Winery Passport—I got mine! You can get yours by requesting it from their Web site at www.gotexanwine.org (click on the Passport link). A winery is a wonderful destination location for business meetings, parties, weddings, receptions or whatever the event (okay, that kid thing again—perhaps not their birthday parties). It's the perfect place to meet up with a few friends or family members or the ideal spot to take a date. Who knows, for the price of a bottle of wine you might even fall in love. How perfect is that! ★

This couple stopped to relax on the patio at Becker Vineyards on their way home from a camping trip to the Frio River

37

Growing Grapes

I love to dig in the dirt and I've nurtured a vegetable garden almost every year out of the past twenty-five. I even grew grapes for several years in the backyard at our former house. But it was on a small scale, mainly for fun and a way to shade our kids' swing set that we put under an arbor. I'm inspired to grow grapes again now that I have plenty of space and am a bit more educated about the process. But I don't think that I could grow grapes with the intention of making a living at it. With the huge risks involved, many which are beyond anyone's control, it's a wonder that anyone tackles the challenge of starting a vineyard. As for any Texas farmer, whether growing grapes, cotton, or any other crop, success doesn't come easily, and it can't be a part-time job. But, luckily for the rest of us, there are folks all over the state that make the commitment of their time, energy, and money to pursue their dreams. Many of the vintners that I talked to have had to replant after complete devastation of their vineyards by Pierce's disease (caused by the bacterium Xylella fastidiosa which is spread by a group of insects known as sharpshooters) or from late freezes, and they've done just that—replanted. That takes persistence and faith. But grape growing can be profitable, and the demand for Texas-grown

Grapevine growing in the Esco's backyard circa 1990

grapes has skyrocketed with all the new wineries that are popping up. This is good news for the large commercial farming operations and small vineyards alike. It's motivation for me.

Figuring out which grapes to plant can be a daunting task, and the consequences of these choices have the potential to make or break a vintner. And that's only one part of the equation. There are a number challenges to growing grapes which need careful consideration and the best solutions for success: how to irrigate; how to recognize disease, and how to prevent it; how to control weeds and pests; and how to prune the vines. However, the TDA, over the past several years, has implemented programs to educate prospective winemakers to aid them in making such important decisions. The Texas Winegrape Network (http://winegrapes.tamu. edu), a joint effort by Texas A&M University and the Texas AgriLife Extension Service is a valuable resource for grape farmers. There is even a grape growing and winemaking degree offered through the Viticulture and Enology program at Grayson County College outside Sherman. Aspiring vintners can choose between an Associate of Applied Science degree that requires sixty-five course hours or a thirty-one-hour certificate program. Classes are taught at the T.V. Munson Viticulture and Enology Center located at the college, a 5,000-square-foot facility that includes a library, classrooms, and labs for processing grapes to make juice and wine. Under the direction of

T.V. Munson Memorial Vineyard at Grayson County College

Roy E. Renfro, Jr., PhD, it is home to the T. V. Munson Memorial.

Not only is it a good idea to be educated in the process of winemaking but it helps to have experience in farming or to hire someone who does. Grape growing is labor intensive, and the key component in maintaining a successful vineyard is the people who work in it. The job requires a serious commitment of time, energy, and efforts. Grapes, like some women, are high-maintenance; it takes a lot of time to train and prune the vines, check for disease, eliminate pests, keep out the weeds, water consistently, and harvest. As with any production line, whether you're making books or wine, each person in the process has to do

41

the job correctly in order for the people down the line to do theirs. The collaborative efforts from the owner to the farmer to the winemaker to the tasting room server (and sometimes it's all the same person) are necessary for success and from whose very fruits bear the reputation of each.

When dealing in real estate you know the saying, it's all about location, location, location.

This is especially true in the grape-growing business. And if you're growing grapes in Texas, that's a lot of location. Conditions have to be just right to grow grapes successfully. The soil, the climate, and the water all determine whether or not a particular variety will thrive in a certain area. Location also determines the amount of grapes harvested and the quality of the fruit. There are eight federally approved viticulture areas in Texas and, although they are somewhat determined by region, the designation simply means that a minimum of eighty-five percent of a wine's grapes must be grown in that particular viticulture in order to be labeled from that area. They are The Bell Mountain Viticultural Area, established in 1986; Fredericksburg in the Texas Hill Country Viticultural Area, established in 1988; Texas Hill Country Viticultural Area, established in 1991; Escondido Valley Viticultural Area, established in 1992; Texas High Plains Viticultural Area, established in 1993; Davis Mountain Viticultural Area, established in 1999; Mesilla Valley Viticultural Area, established in 1985; and Texoma Viticultural Area, established in 1992. For more information about these Texas grape growing regions, visit the Web site http://txwineregions.tamu.edu. (See p. 58 for a map.)

Vineyard worker at Fall Creek Vineyards near Tow

If you're looking for land to purchase to start a vineyard, then you must consider the type of wine you want to make as a determining factor in which viticulture you shop. And if you already own the land, then you must consider the viticulture as a determining factor in the type of vine that you plant. Either way, the viticulture area in which a vineyard is located has everything to do with deciding which varieties to grow. Remember your history lesson: plant native vines for the best results. Otherwise you may be sunk before you ever harvest a single grape. There is no shortage of resources for grape growers in this state. The professionals are out there, and with all of the research and experiments going with the different grape varieties, their insights are invaluable. Planting the wrong grapes, which is doomsday for a winery, can be avoided. Currently, the single biggest threat to grape production in Texas is Pierce's disease. There is a huge effort by a number of institutions coordinating with the Texas A&M University System to understand and ultimately control this devastating disease, for which TAMU has established the Texas Pierce's Disease Research Laboratory and Vineyard at Fredericksburg. Texas is not relying on France to repay Munson's favor.

Grapevines generally are sold as dormant, bare-rooted plants. Grapes are self-fruitful which means they need no pollination and most are grafted—the vine is started with a cutting from one variety that is then connected to another variety by a horticultural process called grafting. The resulting rootstocks are resistant to certain pathogens. The variety of the grape

determines the variety of the wine. The quality of the grape determines the quality of the wine but there's also more to it than that. Every single element in the process will influence the quality. The type of soil, the mineral content of the water, the timing of the harvest all affect the outcome of the wine long before the actual fermentation process even begins.

In addition to deadly diseases that destroy entire vineyards there's also the extreme Texas weather. People living in the state for any length of time are familiar with winter or late

Vineyards at Barking Rocks Winery and Vineyard near Granbury

45

freezes, hailstorms, and drought or excessive rainfall and flooding. And there are the birds, like crows, and small mammals, like raccoons and opossums, that wreak havoc. Many vineyards are surrounded by game fences that are tall enough to keep out deer. The first thing Mark noticed when we drove up to Luz de Estrella outside Marfa was how low the fence is compared to many of the ones in the Hill Country. And while I had noticed a couple of pronghorns nearby when we drove past the vineyard earlier, it wasn't until we questioned the height of the fence that we learned the pronghorns keep the deer out of the vineyard with their speed (the second-fastest animal in the world after the cheetah), but they can't jump the fence to gain entry to the vineyard.

Irrigation is critical. Grapes are mostly water and with the extremes in weather, especially when it comes to rain, mechanical irrigation is a requirement. Most vines are watered by a simple drip system that supplies water to the roots. This is the most effective way to irrigate. Overhead watering is a no-no as this method promotes disease. If watering is the most critical component to a good crop, pruning is second. There is a scientific method to follow when establishing a vineyard and pruning is also necessary in subsequent years. Even for a home gardener, pruning makes all the difference when growing grapes.

With all the challenges and risks, the grape growing business in Texas is thriving.

Vineyards and porch of the tasting room at McReynolds Wines near Cypress Mill

New vineyards are on the rise and existing ones are often planting new vines. There are a number of commercial operations around the state that sell their grapes to the smaller vineyards. Demand is high and many wineries sign contractual agreements ahead of time to ensure they get the grape supply they need to supplement their own harvest.

If everything goes well, if pestilence and disease are successfully controlled, if the crops are protected from predators, if the

Viiew of
Bluff Dale Vineyards
near Bluff Dale

weather permits, then harvesting is the reward. Mechanical harvesting is a necessity for the larger commercial operations with vineyards covering acres and acres of land but it is hardly affordable for smaller ventures. Hand picking grapes is time consuming. I remember one year when we harvested the arbor vine—my children, Elissa and Kyle, along with their cousin Anthony spent the better part of the day picking all the grapes they could find for only a few bowls of fruit. When you consider that it takes about 800 grapes to make a single bottle of wine, that's a whole lot of picking.

But as time-intensive a task it is, this method of harvesting grapes is the best for ensuring that the most grapes are gathered while sustaining the least amount of damage to the fruit. I wouldn't advise hiring two nine-year-olds and a five-year-old for the job but rather assign the task to more experienced and gentle hands as it is a crucial link in the wine production chain. Similarly, proper timing of the harvest is a critical factor in the resulting quality of the finished wine. In Texas, grapes begin to ripen in mid- to late-summer, depending upon their location. Close daily monitoring of the vines is necessary not only to determine the optimum time to harvest but also to watch for signs of predators that would love to devour a nice ripe vineyard. ★

Vines at Alamosa Wine Cellars near Bend

49

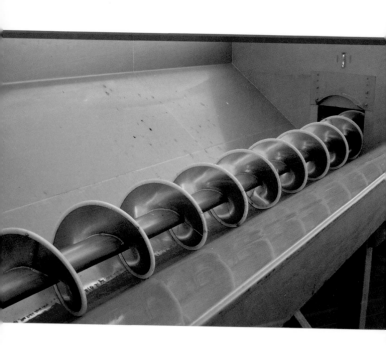

Making Wine

When most people, young or old, think about winemaking, they can't help but conjure up that iconic image of Lucy Ricardo with "feet as large as pizzas" stomping grapes in the 1956 *I Love Lucy* episode. I think this is why it is a popular event at wineries. I've not witnessed a real live grape stomp first hand and truth be told, I won't even consider attending one lest I get that image stuck in my head. I don't want your feet in my wine! Luckily for me and for you, Texas winemakers aren't actually crushing their grapes that way. There are big, industrial stainless steel pieces of equipment that do it for them automatically, and in a sterile environment, thank you very much. This is the first step of the process and it's what separates the juice from the skins, seed and stems.

The type of wine bottled depends upon the variety of the grape. The Texas red varietals include Malbec, Tempranillo, Syrah, Sangiovese, Zinfandel, Merlot, Cabernet Sauvignon, Pino Noir, and Lenoir. The Texas white varietals are Chardonnay, Blanc du Bois, Pinot Grigio, Voignier, Riesling, Sauvignon Blanc, Chenin Blanc, Gewurztraminer, and Semillon. The juice from all of the varietals, red or white, is essentially the same color. Wine gets its color from how long the skins of the grapes soak in the juice during fermentation. Leaving the skins

Grape crushing machine at Llano Estacado Winery near Lubbock

in for a short amount of time results in a blush wine, while leaving them in for an extended period yields the reds. The skins are separated immediately from the crushed grapes when processing white wine. Grape skins contain a compound called reservatrol that accounts for wine's anti-oxidant properties. Therefore, red wine, which contains the most, offers the greatest health benefits.

After crushing the grapes, the clear juice is allowed to settle. It is then separated from the sediment in a process called racking whereby the juice is pumped out of one container into another. Next yeast is added—it's what turns grape juice into wine. Yeast is a spore that feeds on the sugars in the grape juice. This is the organic process of fermentation when the sugars are converted into alcohol and carbon dioxide. Fermentation takes place in large steel vats that are monitored closely by measuring the sugar content of samples of the juice and through taste and smell. There is much more science involved in the process than I'll expand on here but this is also where the fine art of winemaking comes into play.

The next step in making wine is clarification. This is simply a filtration process in which sulfur dioxide is added to the fermented juice to protect the wine against oxidation that leads to microbial spoilage. Most reds don't need to undergo a clarification process but they do go through a fining process to remove tannins. (Look it up in the glossary.) But white wines

Fermentation vats at Llano Estacado Winery

and blush wines require both filtration and fining or they will not be totally clear. Again, the skill of the winemaker is challenged. It is important to achieve the desired clarity of the wine without sacrificing taste and smell.

Stabilizing the wine comes next. White wines go through a hot stabilization process to remove excess protein and also cold stabilization since they are usually served cold. This part of

the process prevents tartrate crystals from form-ing. The quality of wine is strongly affected by stabilization processes so the winemaker must achieve stability without over-processing.

Barrel room at
Cap*Rock Winery
near Lubbock

The aging process really affects the quality of a wine. Wine is first aged in barrels, and red wines are often aged in the bottle after that. Most winemakers use barrels milled from 110-year-old French oak trees. (I learned this on Adam's guided tour featuring the barrel exhibit at the Llano Estacado Winery). Each barrel typically holds sixty gallons of wine which when full weighs about 600 pounds. When I think about how a barrel is made, using just thin strips of wood, I wonder how they can support that much weight when stacked on top of each other. Sometimes the barrel is "toasted" or charred on the inside to give the wine an added flavor. The wine may be racked again a time or two in the barrels during the aging process.

Next comes bottling. The Texas Alcoholic Beverage Commission (TABC) enforces strict guidelines for this process. The bottling area of a winery must meet required standards, and no bottles can be reused. Bottles can be capped with either a cork or an "alternate closure"—Bobby Smith's term for a screw top cap. Corking is the much more expensive option but screw tops carry a stigma that can influence a customer's

Owner Linda Armstrong filling an order at Luz de Estrella Winery near Marfa

perception about a wine's quality. Whether or not the type of closure used affects the taste of the wine inside the bottle is debatable. TABC mandates the bottles must be sealed in such a way that the seal must be broken in order to open the wine.

There are so many varied and interesting labels found on bottles of Texas wine that they alone could fill this book. Behind every trademark design there is a story. Some were commissioned to professional designers who consider branding as much a science as an art. Others were created by a friend or family member, each an artist in his or her own right. The logos, some minimal, some extremely detailed, speak to the spirit of the winery owners. While the identifying artwork is important in marketing wine to the consumer, the trademark is not the only thing that appears on a wine label. Strict laws govern the labeling of wine and all labels must be approved by the TABC as well as by the U. S. Bureau of Alcohol, Tobacco, and Firearms. In addition to the trademark or brand name of the winery, every label must include the name and location of the winery that produces and bottles the wine. The name of the wine can be varietal for wines that contain at least seventy-five percent of wine from the named variety. For varietally labeled wines it is mandatory that the appellation or geographic region be identified and the grapes used in the wine must come from that region. A wine name can also be generic or proprietary if the

Label for Texas Hills' 2005 Kick Butt Cab

wine is made from several types of grapes. The label must also carry the wine's percentage of alcohol. If a wine contains less than fourteen percent alcohol it may be labeled "Table Wine" thus leaving off the exact amount of alcohol it contains. The label has to show the quantity of wine in the bottle—this is measured in liters or milliliters. The vintage date on a bottle of wine indicates the year that the grapes were harvested and fermentation began. If the vintage date is omitted it means that the wine was blended using more than one year's harvest. Just like a book's cover, I wonder how many bottles of wine are bought by customers who judge the wine simply by its label. ★

Texas Viticultural Areas

Areas drawn according to the Federal Register Section that established the American Viticultural Areas.

✦ **Texas High Plains**

✦ **Texoma** • Montague, Cook, Grayson & Fannin counties

✦ **Mesilla Valley** • north & west of El Paso into New Mexico

✦ **Texas Hill Country**

✦ **Escondido Valley** east of Fort Stockton

✦ **Texas Davis Mountains**

✦ **Bell Mountain** •14 miles northeast of Fredericksburg off Hwy 16

✦ **Fredericksburg** in the Texas Hill Country

58

Texas Wineries

Following is a list of all of the wineries that are currently operating in Texas with the physical address and phone number of each location as well as available email and Web site addresses. This list is courtesy of the Texas Department of Agriculture and is grouped by region as published in the department's Texas Winery Guide. Due to space limitations in this book the maps, descriptions, and visiting hours for each winery found in the TDA's guide have been omitted.

Central Region

ALAMOSA WINE CELLARS
677 County Road 430, P.O. Box 212. Bend TX 76824
Winery: (325) 628-3313   Austin: (512) 335-0051 ext. 103
www.alamosawinecellars.com

BECKER VINEYARDS
464 Becker Farms Road, Stonewall TX 78671
(830) 644-2681   Fax: (830) 644-2689
E-mail: beckervyds@beecreek.net   www.beckervineyards.com

BELL MOUNTAIN VINEYARDS
463 Bell Mountain Road, Fredericksburg TX 78624
(830) 685-3297
E-mail: contactus@bellmountainwine.com
www.bellmountainwine.com

THE BELLA VISTA RANCH
3101 Mount Sharp Road, Wimberley TX 78676
(512) 847-6514
E-mail: oliveguy@bvranch.com   www.bvranch.com

Brennan Vineyards
802 South Austin Street, Comanche TX 76442
(325) 356-9100   Fax: (325) 356-5556   Cell: (325) 330-0878
E-mail: tina@brennanvineyards.com   www.brennanvineyards.com

Chisholm Trail Winery
2367 Usener Road, P.O. Box 1274, Fredericksburg TX 78624
(830) 990-CORK (2675) or (877) 990-2675
Fax: (830) 990-9965   E-mail: chisholmtrail@beecreek.net
www.chisholmtrailwinery.com

Comfort Cellars Winery
723 Front Street, P.O. Box 324, Comfort TX 78013
Phone and Fax: (830) 995-3274   E-mail: cathie@hctc.net

Driftwood Vineyards
4001 Elder Hill Road, Driftwood TX 78619
(512) 692-6229 or (512) 858-9667
Fax: (512) 858-2020   E-mail: info@driftwoodvineyards.com
www.driftwoodvineyards.com

Dry Comal Creek
1741 Herbelin Road, New Braunfels TX 78132
(830) 885-4076   Fax: (830) 885-4124
E-mail: inquire@drycomalcreek.com   www.drycomalcreek.com

Fall Creek Vineyards
1820 County Road 222, Tow TX 78672
(Vineyard, Winery and Event Center) (325) 379-5361
Business Office: 1402 San Antonio Street, Suite 200
Austin TX 78701
(512) 476-4477   Fax: (512) 476-6116
E-mail: chad@fcv.com   www.fcv.com

FAWN CREST VINEYARDS
1370 Westside Circle, Canyon Lake TX 78133
(830) 935-2407 or (281) 413-2045
E-mail: fawncrest@hotmail.com   www.fawncrest.com

FLAT CREEK ESTATE
24912 Singleton Bend East, Marble Falls TX 78654
(Located off 1431, 6 miles west of Lago Vista)
(512) 267-6310 or (512) 267-1802
Fax: (512) 267-6321   E-mail: wines@flatcreekestate.com
www.flatcreekestate.com

FREDERICKSBURG WINERY
247 West Main Street, Fredericksburg TX 78624
(830) 990-8747   Fax: (830) 990-8566
E-mail: wine@fbgwinery.com   www.fbgwinery.com

GRAPE CREEK VINEYARDS
10587 East Hwy 290, Fredericksburg TX 78624
(830) 644-2710
E-mail: relax@grapecreek.com   www.grapecreek.com

LA CRUZ DE COMAL WINES, LTD.
7405 FM 2722, Startzville TX 78133
(830) 899-2723
E-mail: ld3@gvtc.com   www.lacruzdecomalwines.com

LOST CREEK VINEYARD
1129 Ranch Road 2233, Sunrise Beach TX 78643
(325) 388-3753   Tasting Room: 302 East Main Street
Johnson City TX 78636
E-mail: lcvine@moment.net
www.lostcreekvineyard.com

MANDOLA ESTATE WINERY
13308 FM 150 West, Driftwood TX 78619
(512) 858-1470   Fax: (512) 858-1340
E-mail: info@mandolawines.com   www.mandolawines.com

McREYNOLDS WINES
706 Shovel Mountain Road, Cypress Mill TX 78663
(830) 825-3544   Fax: (830) 825-1105
E-mail: mcreynoldswines@hillcountrytx.net
www.mcreynoldswines.com

PEDERNALES CELLARS
2916 Upper Albert Rd., Stonewall TX 78761
(830) 644-2037   Fax: (866) 548-7940
E-mail: info@pedernalescellars.com   www.pedernalescellars.com

PERISSOS VINEYARDS AND WINERY
7214 Park Road 4 W, Burnet TX 78611
(512) 656-8419   Fax: (512) 715-0212
www.perissosvineyards.com

PILLAR BLUFF VINEYARDS
300 County Road 111, Lampasas TX 76550
(512) 556-4078   Fax: (512) 556-4078
E-mail: vineyard@earth-comm.com   www.pillarbluff.com

POTEET COUNTRY WINERY
400 Tank Hollow Road, Poteet TX 78065
(830) 276-8085
E-mail: bobbydenson@msn.com   www.poteetwine.com

RANCHO PONTE VINEYARD
315 Ranch Road 1376, Fredericksburg TX 78624
(830) 990-8555   Fax: (830) 990-8555
E-mail: info@ranchoponte.com   www.ranchoponte.com

Rising Star Vineyards
1001 County Road 290, Rising Star TX 76471
(254) 643-1776 or (512) 899-9882   Fax: (512) 251-5548
E-mail: moubre@txwinemark.com   www.risingstarvineyards.com

Sandstone Cellars Winery
211 San Antonio Street, P.O. Box 1246, Mason TX 76856
(325) 347-9463
E-mail: wine@sandstonecellarswinery.com
www.sandstonecellarswinery.com

Singing Water Vineyards
316 Mill Dam Road, Comfort TX 78013
(830) 995-2246   E-mail: singingwater@omniglobal.net
www.singingwatervineyards.com

Sister Creek Vineyards
1142 Sisterdale Road, Sisterdale TX 78006
(12 miles north of Boerne on FM 1376 or
17 miles south of US Hwy 290)
(830) 324-6704   Fax: (830) 324-6704
E-mail: sistercreek@hctc.net   www.sistercreekvineyards.com

Spicewood Vineyards
1419 County Road 409, P.O. Box 248, Spicewood TX 78669
(830) 693-5328   Fax: (830) 693-5940
E-mail: wines@spicewoodvineyards.com
www.spicewoodvineyards.com

Stone House Vineyard
24350 Haynie Flat Road, Spicewood TX 78669
(512) 264-3630 or (512) 264-9890   Fax: (512) 264-9759
E-mail: info@stonehousevineyard.com
www.stonehousevineyard.com

Texas Hills Vineyard
878 Ranch Road 2766, P.O. Box 1480
Johnson City TX 78636
(830) 868-2321   Fax: (830) 868-7027
E-mail: wine@texashillsvineyard.com   www.texashillsvineyard.com

Texas Legato
2935 FM 1478, Lampasas TX 76550 (512) 556-9600
E-mail: bill.bledsoe@tx.rr.com   www.texaslegato.com

Three Dudes Winery
125 Old Martindale Road, San Marcos TX 78666
(512) 392-5634
E-mail: dudes@threedudeswinery.com
www.threedudeswinery.com

Torre Di Pietra Winery
10915 East Hwy 290, Fredericksburg TX 78624
P.O. Box 1727, Fredericksburg TX 78624
(830) 644-2829   Fax: (830) 644-2830
E-mail: tdp@beecreek.net
www.texashillcountrywine.com

Wimberley Valley Winery at Driftwood
2825 Lone Man Mountain Road, Driftwood TX 78619
(512) 847-2592
E-mail: wvwtr@yahoo.com   www.wimberleyvalleywines.com

Woodrose Winery
662 Woodrose Lane, Stonewall TX 78671 (830) 644-2539
E-mail: greatwines@woodroseswinery.com
www.woodrosewinery.com

Northern Region

ARCHÉ
228 Wagner Road, Saint Jo TX 76265
(214) 908-9055   Fax: (972) 701-0968
E-mail: GoodWines@ArcheWines.com   www.ArcheWines.com

BARKING ROCKS WINERY & VINEYARD
1919 Allen Court, Granbury TX 76048 (817) 579-0007
E-mail: tiberia@barkingrockswine.com
www.barkingrockswine.com

THE BLUE ARMADILLO WINERY
2702 Lee Street, Greenville TX 75401 (903) 455-WINE (9463)
www.bluearmadillowinery.com

BLUE ROOSTER WINERY
606 West Pine Street (U.S. Hwy 80) Edgewood TX 75117
(903) 896-4588   Fax: (903) 896-2538
E-mail: bluerooster@sbcglobal.net

BLUFF DALE VINEYARDS
5222 County Road 148, Bluff Dale TX 76433
P.O. Box 110, Bluff Dale TX 76433
(254) 728-3540   Fax: (254) 728-3541
E-mail: bluffdalevines@lipan.net   www.bluffdalevineyards.com

BRUSHY CREEK VINEYARDS AND WINERY
572 County Road 2798, Alvord TX 76225 (50 miles NW of Fort
Worth on CR 2798 at US 287/81 between Decatur & Bowie TX)
(940) 427-4747 or (817) 821-0175
E-mail: brushyck@wf.net   www.brushycreekvineyards.com

CALAIS WINERY
3000 Commerce Street, Dallas TX 75226
(214) 453-2548
E-mail: bcs@calaiswinery.com
www.calaiswinery.com

COLLIN OAKS WINERY
6874 County Road 398, Princeton TX 75407
(214) 504-9701   E-mail: thefolks@collinoakswinery.com
www.collinoakswinery.com

CROSS TIMBERS WINERY
805 North Main Street, Grapevine TX 76051
(817) 488-6789   Fax: (817) 488-7981
E-mail: crosstimberswinery@directlink.net
www.crosstimberswinery.com

CROSSROADS WINERY
15222 King Road #301, Frisco TX 75034
(972) 294-4144 or (214) 725-5646
Fax: (972) 899-1295
E-mail: john@friscowinery.com
www.friscowinery.com

DELANEY VINEYARDS AT GRAPEVINE
2000 Champagne Blvd., Grapevine TX 76051
(817) 481-5668   Fax: (817) 251-8119
E-mail: info@delaneyvineyards.com   www.delaneyvineyards.com

ENOCH'S STOMP VINEYARD AND WINERY
870 Ferguson Rd (FM 4312), Harleton TX 75651
(903) 736-9494   Fax: (903) 663-8725
E-mail: info@enochsstomp.com   www.enochstomp.com

FUQUA WINERY
3737 Atwell St., Suite #203, Dallas TX 75209
(214) 769-1147
E-mail: lee@fuquawinery.com   www.fuquawinery.com

GRAYSON HILLS WINERY
2815 Ball Road, Whitewright TX 75491
(903) 627-0832   www.graysonhillswinery.com

HOMESTEAD WINERY AT IVANHOE
Production Facility: P.O. Box 35, Ivanhoe TX 75447
(903) 583-4281   Fax: (903) 583-2024
www.homesteadwinery.com

HOMESTEAD WINERY AT DENISON
Wine Tasting Facility: 220 West Main Street, Denison TX 75020
(903) 464-0030
www.homesteadwinery.com

HOMESTEAD WINERY AT GRAPEVINE
Wine Tasting Facility: 211 East Worth, Grapevine TX 76051
(817) 251-9463
www.homesteadwinery.com

INWOOD ESTATES VINEYARDS
1350 Manufacturing St. #209, Dallas TX 75207
(214) 902-9452 or (214) 679-1907
Fax: (214) 902-9452
E-mail: getinfo@inwoodwines.com   www.inwoodwines.com

KE CELLARS
4574 South Broadway, Tyler TX 75703
(903) 939-9805   Fax: (903) 939-9510
E-mail: info@kecellars.com   www.kecellars.com

KHATTER VINEYARDS
4110 Brookwood Drive, Parker TX 75002
(972) 516-1940
E-mail: carolyn_khatter@tx.rr.com   www.khattervineyards.com

KIEPERSOL ESTATES VINEYARDS
3933 FM 344 East, Tyler TX 75703
(903) 894-8995   Fax: (903) 894-7933
E-mail: winery@kiepersol.com   www.kiepersol.com

LA BODEGA WINERY
Dallas/Fort Worth International Airport
Terminal A, Gate A15, Terminal D, Gate D14,
DFW Airport TX 75261
(972) 574-1440 (A15) or (972) 973-WINE (D14)
Fax: (817) 421-2495
E-mail: hpuente@pbedfw.com   www.labodegawinery.com

LA BUENA VIDA VINEYARDS AT GRAPEVINE
416 East College Street, Grapevine TX 76051
(817) 481-WINE (9463)   Fax: (817) 421-3635
E-mail: Tasting Room: adam@labuenavida.com
Event Booking: events@labuenavida.com
www.labuenavida.com

LA BUENA VIDA VINEYARDS AT SPRINGTOWN
650 Vineyard Lane, Springtown TX 76082
(817) 220-4366
www.labuenavida.com

LANDON WINERY
101 North Kentucky Street, McKinney TX 75069
(972) 542-3030
E-mail: winery@landonwinery.com   www.landonwinery.com

LIGHTCATCHER WINERY
6925 Confederate Park Road/FM1886
Fort Worth TX 76108
(817) 237-2626   Fax: (817) 237-1629
E-mail: info@lightcatcher.com   www.lightcatcher.com

LONE OAK WINERY
2116 FM 731, Burleson TX 76028
(817) 426-6625   Fax: (817) 426-2334
E-mail: info@loneoakwinery.com
www.loneoakwinery.com

LONE STAR WINE CELLARS
103 East Virginia Street Suite 104
McKinney TX 75069
(972) 547-WINE(9463)
www.lonestarwinecellars.com

LOS PINOS RANCH VINEYARDS
658 County Road 1334, Pittsburg TX 75686
(903) 855-1769   Fax: (903) 855-1771
E-mail: info@lospinosranchvineyards.com
www.lospinosranchvineyards.com

LOUVINEY WINERY & RESTAURANT
206 Main Street, Sulphur Springs TX 75482
(903) 438-8320
E-mail: louvineys@louviney.com   www.louviney.com

MAYDELLE COUNTRY WINES
175 CR 2108, Rusk TX 75785
(903) 795-3915
E-mail: sales@maydellewines.com   www.maydellewines.com

PARIS VINEYARDS
545 County Road 43500, Paris TX 75462
(903) 785-WINE (9463)
E-mail: denise@parisvineyards.com   www.parisvineyards.com

PARIS VINEYARDS WINERY ON THE SQUARE
2 Clarksville Street, Paris TX 75460
(903) 785-WINE (9463)
E-mail: denise@parisvineyards.com   www.parisvineyards.com

RED CABOOSE WINERY
1147 CR 1110, Meridian TX 76665
(254) 435-9911 or (214) 415-4843
Fax: (254) 435-9910
E-mail: garyredcaboose@hotmail.com
www.redcaboosewinery.com

RED ROAD VINEYARD AND WINERY
105 West Front Street, Naples TX 75568
(903) 897-9353   Fax: (903) 897-9353
E-mail: rrvw105w@yahoo.com   www.redroadvineyard.com

SAN MARTI~NO WINERY AND VINEYARD
12512 Hwy 205, Rockwall TX 75087
Mailing Address: P.O. Box 2229 Rockwall TX 75087
(972) 772-6043   Fax: (972) 772-1902
E-mail: winery@sanmartinowinery.com
www.sanmartinowinery.com

SAVANNAH WINERY & BISTRO
574 East Highway 64, Canton TX 75103
(903) 567-6810 or (903) 714-4097   Fax: (903) 567-6810
E-mail: savannahwinerytx@aol.com   www.savannahwinerytx.com

St. Rose Vineyard and Winery
2170 County Road 4110, Pittsburg TX 75686
(469) 744-1661   E-mail: st.rosewinery@gmail.com
www.guerravineyardandwinery.com

Sunset Winery
1535 South Burleson Boulevard Burleson TX 76028
(817) 426-1141 Bruce cell: (817) 891-108
sunset.winery.mail@sbcglobal.net   www.sunsetwinery.com

Sweet Dreams Winery
2549 Anderson County Rd 44, Palestine TX 75803
(903) 549-2027   Fax: (903) 723-0953
E-mail: sweetdreamswinery@yahoo.com
www.sweetdreamswinery.com

Tara Vineyard & Winery
8603 County Road 3914, Athens TX 75752
(903) 675-7023 or (214) 317-9708
E-mail: sipoftexas@tarawinery.com
www.tarawinery.com

Texas Vineyard and Smokehaus
2442 Anderson County Road 2133, Palestine TX 75801
(903) 538-2950   Fax: (903) 538-2950
E-mail: texasvineyard@embarqmail.com

Texoma Winery
9 Judge Carr Road, Whitewright TX 75491
(903) 364-5242   Fax: (903) 364-2207
E-mail: bob.white@texomawinery.com
www.texomawinery.com

Times Ten Cellars
6324 Prospect Avenue, Dallas TX 75214
(214) 824-9463   Fax: (214) 824-9464
E-mail: kert@timestencellars.com   www.timestencellars.com

Triple "R" Ranch & Winery
2276 County Road 125, Whitesboro TX 76243
(214) 850-4020   www.thetriplerranch.com

Wales Manor Winery & Vineyard
4488 County Road 408, McKinney TX 75071
(972) 542-0417
E-mail: wales@walesmanor.com   www.walesmanor.com

Weinhof Winery
16678 FM 455, Forestburg TX 76239
(940) 964-2552
E-mail: brendat@weinhofwinery.com
www.weinhofwinery.com

Western Region

Bar Z Wines
19290 FM 1541, Canyon TX 79015
Mailing Address: P.O. Box 1080, Canyon, TX 79015
(806) 733-2673   Fax: (806) 214-0190
E-mail: barzwines@amaonline.com   www.barzwines.com

Cap*Rock Winery
408 East Woodrow Road, Lubbock TX 79424
(806) 863-2704
E-mail: droark@caprockwinery.com   www.caprockwinery.com

Delaney Vineyards at Lamesa
One mile north of Lamesa on Highway 137, Lamesa TX 79331
(806) 872-3177   Fax: (806) 872-2421
E-mail: info@delaneyvineyards.com   www.delaneyvineyards.com

La Diosa Cellars
901 17th Street, Lubbock TX 79401
(806) 744-3600   Fax: (806) 744-3704
www.ladiosacellars.com

Llano Estacado Winery
P.O. Box 3487, Lubbock TX 79452
(806) 745-2258   Fax: (806) 748-1674
E-mail: info@llanowine.com   www.llanowine.com
Sales & Marketing: 6222 Colleyville Blvd. Suite B,
Colleyville TX 76034
(817) 329-3890 Fax: (817) 421-0919
E-mail: llanoestacado@verizon.net

Luz de Estrella Vineyards
P.O. Box 578, 100 Starlight Lane, East US Hwy 90
Marfa TX 79843
(432) 729-3434   Fax: (432) 729-1819
E-mail: linda@luzdeestrella.com   www.luzdeestrella.com

McPherson Cellars
1615 Texas Avenue, Lubbock TX 79401 (806) 687-WINE
Fax: (806) 687-7919   www.mcphersoncellars.com

Pheasant Ridge Winery
3507 East County Road 5700, Lubbock TX 79403
(806) 746-6033   Fax: (806) 746-6750
E-mail: billgipson@aol.com   www.pheasantridgewinery.com

Star Canyon Winery
2601 North Stanton Street, El Paso TX 79902
(915) 544-7000   Fax: (915) 544-7003
E-mail: dalba02@yahoo.com   www.starcanyonwinery.com

Ste. Genevieve Wines
P.O. Box 130, Fort Stockton TX 79735
(432) 395-2417   Fax: (432) 395-2431

Val Verde Winery
100 Qualia Drive, Del Rio TX 78840
(830) 775-9714   Fax: (830) 775-5394
E-mail: info@valverdewinery.com   www,valverdewinery.com

Zin Valle Vineyards
7315 Hwy 28, Canutillo TX 79835
(915) 877-4544   Fax: (915) 877-2257
E-mail: owners@zinvalle.com   www.zinvalle.com

Southeast Region

Bernhardt Winery
9043 County Road 204, Plantersville TX 77363
(936) 520-8684 or (936) 894-9829
www.bernhardtwinery.com

Bruno & George Wines
400 Messina Road, Sour Lake TX 77659
(409) 963-8235 or (409) 898-2829
E-mail: shawn@brunoandgeorge.com or
misha@brunoandgeorge.com

Circle S Vineyards
9920 Highway 90A #B-268, Sugar Land TX 77478
(281) 265-9463   Fax: (281) 325-0631
E-mail: info@circlesvineyards.com   www.circlesvineyards.com

Colony Cellars
35955 Richard Frey Road, Waller TX 77484
(979) 826-3995 or (979) 826-3073   Fax: (979) 826-3073
E-mail: info@colonycellars.com   www.colonycellars.com

Haak Vineyards & Winery
6310 Avenue T, Santa Fe TX 77510
(409) 925-1401
E-mail: raymond@haakwine.com   www.haakwine.com

Messina Hof Winery & Resort
4545 Old Reliance Road, Bryan TX 77808
(979) 778-9463 or (800) 736-9463   Fax: (979) 778-1729
E-mail: wine@messinahof.com   www.messinahof.com

Piney Woods Country Winery & Vineyards
3408 Willow Drive, Orange TX 77632
(409) 883-5408   Fax: (409) 883-5483
E-mail: pineywoods1@gmail.com   www.pineywoodswines.com

Pleasant Hill Winery
1441 Salem Road, Brenham TX 77833
(979) 830-VINE (8463)   Fax: (979) 277-9218
E-mail: texaswines@yahoo.com   www.pleasanthillwinery.com

Purple Possum Winery
5486 Rabun Road, Navasota TX 77868
(936) 825-2830   Fax: (936) 825-2965
purplepossumwinery@gmail.com   www.purplepossumwinery.com

RETREAT HILL WINERY AND VINEYARD
15551 FM 362 Road, Navasota TX 77868
(936) 825-8282   Fax: (888) 392-5309
www.retreathill.com

ROSEMARY'S VINEYARD & WINERY
5521 Hwy 71 East, La Grange TX 78945
(979) 249-2109 or (281) 728-9737   Fax: (979) 249-2106

TEHUACANA CREEK VINEYARDS & WINERY
6826 East Hwy 6, Waco TX 76705
(254) 875-2375
E-mail: info@wacowinery.com   www.wacowinery.com

WIMBERLEY VALLEY WINERY AT OLD TOWN SPRING
Tasting Room: 206 Main Street, Old Town Spring TX 77373
(281) 350-8801   Fax: (281) 288-8298
E-mail: wvwtr@yahoo.com   www.winberlyvalleywines.com

WINDY WINERY
4232 Clover Road, Brenham TX 77833
(979) 836-3252   Fax: (979) 836-4588
E-mail: info@windywinery.net   www.windywinery.net

YEPEZ VINEYARDS
12739 FM 2354, Baytown TX 77520
(281) 573-4139   Fax: (979) 836-3252
E-mail: sales@yepezvineyard.com   www.Yepezvineyard.com

The patio at Alamosa
Wine Cellars

Glossary

The combination of the science of making wine and the art of consuming it presented the opportunity for me to learn some new vocabulary words. The terms I've defined here are my understanding of what they mean. Many of these words or terms may be defined differently by others—these are simply my interpretations.

Acidity – the main acid compounds found in wine are tartaric, malic, lactic and citric, that when properly balanced give wine its desired tartness and taste.

Aging – the time that wine sits in a tank, a barrel, or a bottle to improve its flavor (more in the case of red wines than white).

Appellation – the region where the grapes are grown.

Aroma – the fruity smell of the grape.

Barrel – a cask made from strips of wood held together by metal bands that hold approximately 60 gallons of wine for storage and aging.

Blush wine – the result of removing grape skins from crushed grapes after a shorter period of time than for red wine.

Body – the weight of the wine in the mouth.

Bouquet – the way a wine smells after fermentation and aging.

Breathing – aerating a bottle of red wine (best accomplished by pouring into a decanter) to bring out the bouquet and develop its complexity.

Cap – the thick layer of grape skins that float on top of the vat while red wine is fermenting.

Cork – wine bottle stopper that is made from the outer tissue of the cork oak.

Crisp – a desirable characteristic of white wine, a term that describes a wine with a fresh level of acidity.

Enology – the science of wine production (also spelled oenology).

Fining – a process to remove microscopic elements that can cloud wine and tannins that can cause bitterness. A number of fining agents can be used: activated charcoal, activated carbon, casein, or egg whites among others.

Finish – the flavor and texture that is left in the mouth after a wine has been swallowed.

Labrusca – one of the main North America vine species

Legs – what drips down inside of the glass after swirling the wine; the slower the drip the fuller the body.

Must – the juice of the grape that has just been crushed.

Nose – a term that refers to the smell of a wine.

Phylloxera – a deadly parasite that destroyed nearly all of the vineyards in France in the 1860s.

Pierce's disease – a deadly bacteria that is spread by leafhoppers known as sharpshooters. It has destroyed many grape crops in Texas and infestations of the disease are found in every area in the state.

Racking – the process by which juice is separated from the sediment by pumping it from one container to another.

Sediment – the tart grainy deposit that is sometimes found in older wines. Not necessarily a bad thing since it is the natural separation of acids, tannins, and color pigments and it may indicate a superior wine.

Stabilization – processes (either hot or cold) that use temperature to separate tartaric acid and fine protein particles from the wine to keep it from being cloudy.

Tannin – an astringent compound found in grape skins and seeds (as well as in oak barrels) that provides structure, flavor, texture, and complexity to wine. A wine described as having a tannic grip would cause one's mouth to pucker.

Tar – used to describe the smell of hot tar that can be found in cabernet and zinfandel wines. It's supposed to be a desirable quality.

Tartaric acid – the principal acid found in grapes; it promotes crispness and graceful aging as it is a good preservative. Tartrate crystals can form over time and while harmless they are removed to keep the wine clear.

Toasty – a desirable flavor produced by charring the insides of the oak barrels used in the aging process.

Varietal – the name of the grape.

Vintner – a person who makes wine.

Viticulture – the cultivation of grapes for winemaking.

Vitis vinifera – the varieties of grapes that were imported to North America from Europe.

Acknowledgments

I thank Judy Alter and Susan Petty, my bookmaking partners at TCU Press, for the assignment and their support. I thank Margie Adkins for her design work on this book. I thank Bobby Champion at the Texas Department of Agriculture for helping me obtain electronic files for the listing of wineries. I thank Pam and Gary Spiller, KK McMillan, Daina Bond, Jim Long, and Tamara Radom for visiting wineries with me—wine is better with friends and loved ones. I thank Barbara Stevenson for driving me over 900 miles in three days to visit seventeen wineries and for the good times we had on all of the other road trips and wine tours we took together over the past year. I thank Kate Barrett for hosting us in her home while Barbara and I explored Hill Country wineries. I thank Bobby, Elissa and Blane Curry, Kyle Esco and Michelle Wooley for a rewarding year and for being patient with me while I was busy touring Texas, drinking wine, and writing this book. I thank Mark Esco for turning right to check out the Rising Star Winery that first time, for driving me to wineries all over Texas, and for everything else he does. And I thank Betty Jo Esco from Bangs for Mark. ★

Mark leaving Texas Hills Vineyards near Johnson City

About the author

Melinda Esco is a sixth-generation Texan and has lived all over the state including five towns that begin with the letter A—in alphabetical order. On the morning of her fiftieth birthday she, husband Mark, and friends Tim and Louise Slominsky hiked McKittrick Canyon in the Guadalupe Mountains National Park and that evening Patricia Vonne taught her to play the castanets at the Railroad Blues in Alpine. She graduated from the University of Texas at Arlington with a bachelor of arts degree in journalism. Melinda has enjoyed a long career in publishing and is currently the production manager at TCU Press in Fort Worth. She makes books for a paycheck and grows fruits and vegetables to eat. Melinda is Mom to Elissa and Kyle and GoGo to Blane. She and Mark live southwest of Azle. ★

Texas
Wineries

ISBN 978-0-87565-396-9
Lithocase: $9.95

A TEXAS SMALL BOOK ™

★

Printed in China

ISBN 978-0-87565-396-9

9 780875 653969

50995